Blue Devilology Trivia Challenge

Duke Blue Devils Basketball

Blue Devilology Trivia Challenge

Duke Blue Devils Basketball

Researched by Paul F. Wilson

Paul F. Wilson & Tom P. Rippey III, Editors

Kick The Ball, Ltd

Lewis Center, Ohio

Trivia by Kick The Ball, Ltd

College Football Trivia

Alabama Crimson Tide	Auburn Tigers	Boston College Eagles	Florida Gators
Georgia Bulldogs	LSU Tigers	Miami Hurricanes	Michigan Wolverines
Nebraska Cornhuskers	Notre Dame Fighting Irish	Ohio State Buckeyes	Oklahoma Sooners
Oregon Ducks	Penn State Nittany Lions	Southern Cal Trojans	Texas Longhorns

Pro Football Trivia

Arizona Cardinals	Buffalo Bills	Chicago Bears	Cleveland Browns
Denver Broncos	Green Bay Packers	Indianapolis Colts	Kansas City Chiefs
Minnesota Vikings	New England Patriots	New Orleans Saints	New York Giants
New York Jets	Oakland Raiders	Philadelphia Eagles	Pittsburgh Steelers
San Francisco 49ers	Washington Redskins		

Pro Baseball Trivia

Boston Red Sox	Chicago Cubs	Chicago White Sox	Cincinnati Reds
Detroit Tigers	Los Angeles Dodgers	New York Mets	New York Yankees
Philadelphia Phillies	Saint Louis Cardinals	San Francisco Giants	

College Basketball Trivia

Duke Blue Devils	Georgetown Hoyas	Indiana Hoosiers	Kansas Jayhawks
Kentucky Wildcats	Maryland Terrapins	Michigan State Spartans	North Carolina Tar Heels
Syracuse Orange	UConn Huskies	UCLA Bruins	

Pro Basketball Trivia

Boston Celtics	Chicago Bulls	Detroit Pistons	Los Angeles Lakers
Utah Jazz			

Visit **www.TriviaGameBooks.com** for more details.

Thanks to my lifelong friend, Damon Smith, one of the most avid Blue Devils fans I personally know, for his input on previous editions of this book.

Blue Devilology Trivia Challenge: Duke Blue Devils Basketball; Third Edition 2010

Published by
Kick The Ball, Ltd
8595 Columbus Pike, Suite 197
Lewis Center, OH 43035
www.TriviaGameBooks.com

Designed, Formatted, and Edited by: Paul F. Wilson & Tom P. Rippey III
Researched by: Paul F. Wilson

For information on ordering this book in bulk at reduced prices, please email us at pfwilson@triviagamebooks.com.

International Standard Book Number: 978-1-934372-91-3

Printed and Bound in the United States of America

10 9 8 7 6 5 4 3 2 1

Table of Contents

Dear Friend,

Thank you for purchasing our **Blue Devilology Trivia Challenge** game book!

We have made every attempt to verify the accuracy of the questions and answers contained in this book. However it is still possible that from time to time an error has been made by us or our researchers. In the event you find a question or answer that is questionable or inaccurate, we ask for your understanding and thank you for bringing it to our attention so we may improve future editions of this book. Please email us at tprippey@triviagamebooks.com with those observations and comments.

Have fun playing **Blue Devilology Trivia Challenge**!

Paul & Tom

Paul Wilson & Tom Rippey
Co-Founders, Kick The Ball, Ltd

PS – You can discover more about all of our current trivia game books by visiting www.TriviaGameBooks.com.

Book Format:

There are four quarters, each made up of fifty questions. Each quarter's questions have assigned point values. Questions are designed to get progressively more difficult as you proceed through each quarter, as well as through the book itself. Most questions are in a four-option multiple-choice format so that you will at least have a 25% chance of getting a correct answer for some of the more challenging questions.

We have even added an overtime section in the event of a tie, or just in case you want to keep playing a little longer.

Game Options:

One Player -
To play on your own, simply answer each of the questions in all the quarters, and in the overtime section, if you'd like. Use the Player / Team Score Sheet to record your answers and the quarter Answer Keys to check your answers. Calculate each quarter's points and the total for the game at the bottom of the Player / Team Score Sheet to determine your final score.

Two or More Players –
To play with multiple players decide if you will all be competing with each other individually, or if you will form and play as teams. Each player / team will then have its own Player / Team Score Sheet to record its answer. You can use the quarter Answer Keys to check your answers and to calculate your final scores.

The Player / Team Score Sheets have been designed so that each team can answer all questions or you can divide the questions up in any combination you would prefer. For example, you may want to alternate questions if two players are playing or answer every third question for three players, etc. In any case, simply record your response to your questions in the corresponding quarter and question number on the Player / Team Score Sheet.

A winner will be determined by multiplying the total number of correct answers for each quarter by the point value per quarter, then adding together the final total for all quarters combined. Play the game again and again by alternating the questions that your team is assigned so that you will answer a different set of questions each time you play.

You Create the Game -
There are countless other ways of using *Blue Devilology Trivia Challenge* questions. It is limited only to your imagination. Examples might be using them at your tailgate or other college basketball related party. Players / Teams who answer questions incorrectly may have to perform a required action, or winners may receive special prizes. Let us know what other games you come up with!

Have fun!

1) What season did the nickname Blue Devils become widely associated with Duke?

Answers begin on page 17

    A) 1897-98
    B) 1914-15
    C) 1922-23
    D) 1941-42

2) What are Duke's official team colors?

    A) Dark Blue and White
    B) Royal Blue and White
    C) White and Navy Blue
    D) White and Deep Blue

3) What is the current name of Duke's home basketball arena?

    A) Duke Indoor Stadium
    B) Cameron Indoor Stadium
    C) Horace Trumbauer Pavilion
    D) Julian Abele Arena

4) How many Duke players have been named Naismith College Player of the Year?

    A) 7
    B) 9
    C) 11
    D) None of the above

5) In addition to "Blue & White", which other song is an official Duke fight song?

   A) "Dear Old Duke"
   B) "Fight! Blue Devils, Fight!"
   C) "The Duke Football Song"
   D) "Fight Blue & White!"

6) What is the nickname of the student cheering section at Duke home games?

   A) Blue Devil Crazies
   B) Duke Crazies
   C) Krzyzewski Crazies
   D) Cameron Crazies

7) How many all-time Final Four appearances does Duke have?

   A) 6
   B) 8
   C) 11
   D) 15

8) Who has the longest coaching tenure at Duke?

   A) Mike Krzyzewski
   B) Eddie Cameron
   C) Harold Bradley
   D) Vic Bubas

9) What year did Duke join the ACC?

    A) 1929
    B) 1942
    C) 1953
    D) 1975

10) Who was Duke's head coach for the final 19 games of the 1994-95 season?

    A) Pete Gaudet
    B) Mike Krzyzewski
    C) Bill Foster
    D) Neill McGeachy

11) What year did Duke play its first-ever basketball game?

    A) 1888
    B) 1893
    C) 1900
    D) 1906

12) What is the official capacity of Cameron Indoor Stadium?

    A) 7,365
    B) 7,931
    C) 8,872
    D) 9,314

13) What is the official name of Duke's costumed mascot?

A) The Blue Devil
B) The Little Devil
C) The Devil
D) The Alpine Devil

14) Which broadcaster is currently known as "The Voice of the Blue Devils"?

A) Dick Groat
B) Add Penfield
C) Bob Harris
D) Wes Chesson

15) What was the nickname of the Angier B. Duke Gymnasium?

A) The Ark
B) The Gym
C) The Palace
D) The AB Gym

16) Which non-conference opponent has Duke played the greatest number of times?

A) South Carolina
B) Navy
C) Davidson
D) George Washington

17) Did Duke win its first-ever basketball game?

    A) Yes
    B) No

18) What is the name of the temporary tent city erected outside of Cameron Indoor Stadium?

    A) Krzyzewskiville
    B) Cameron City
    C) Krzyzewskburgh
    D) City O' Tents

19) Who has the second longest coaching tenure at Duke?

    A) Vic Bubas
    B) Gerry Gerard
    C) Bill Foster
    D) Eddie Cameron

20) Who was the first Consensus All-American (First or Second Team) at Duke?

    A) Dick Groat
    B) Art Heyman
    C) Ed Koffenberger
    D) Jeff Mullins

21) Did Duke have a winning record their first-ever season?

A) Yes
B) No

22) Which opponent did Duke play in the most recent non-sellout game played at Cameron Indoor Stadium?

A) Virginia
B) Clemson
C) Boston College
D) Virginia Tech

23) Which coach has the most career wins as Blue Devils head coach?

A) Eddie Cameron
B) Vic Bubas
C) Harold Bradley
D) Mike Krzyzewski

24) What was the highest AP ranking Duke achieved in the 2009-10 season?

A) No. 1
B) No. 3
C) No. 4
D) No. 6

25) Who holds the record for assists in a single game at Duke?

    A)   Bobby Hurley
    B)   Greg Paulus
    C)   Tommy Amaker
    D)   Chris Collins

26) What year was Duke's first-ever unbeaten season?

    A)   1908
    B)   1913
    C)   1923
    D)   None of the above

27) What are Duke's most consecutive NCAA Tournament appearances?

    A)   15
    B)   17
    C)   19
    D)   21

28) The Blue Devils have had greater than five seasons in which they lost only one game.

    A)   True
    B)   False

29) Which ACC opponent has Duke played the greatest number of times?

    A) Wake Forest
    B) North Carolina
    C) N.C. State
    D) Maryland

30) How many winning seasons (excludes .500 seasons) did Duke have its first six seasons?

    A) 2
    B) 3
    C) 5
    D) 6

31) How many seasons has Duke only had one loss at home?

    A) 29
    B) 36
    C) 47
    D) None of the above

32) Against which team did Duke get its all-time first victory?

    A) Wake Forest
    B) Littleton HS
    C) Guilford
    D) Trinity Park

33) What is the total number of seasons the Blue Devils have gone undefeated at home?

A) 14
B) 18
C) 25
D) 29

34) Which of the following is not a current Blue Devils assistant coach?

A) Johnny Dawkins
B) Chris Collins
C) Nate James
D) Steve Wojciechowski

35) What year did Duke's Cameron Indoor Stadium open?

A) 1937
B) 1940
C) 1943
D) 1947

36) Duke led the nation in three-point field goals made in the 2000-01 season?

A) True
B) False

37) Which player holds the record for most points scored in a single game against Duke?

A) Don Hennon
B) Kenny Carr
C) Dickie Hemric
D) Ernie Beck

38) What sport is the subject of "Fight! Blue Devils, Fight!"?

A) Baseball
B) Basketball
C) Football
D) Track and Field

39) What are the fewest field goals a Duke team has allowed in a single game?

A) 4
B) 9
C) 11
D) 16

40) What type of offense does Coach K run at Duke?

A) Set
B) Motion
C) Triangle
D) Zone

41) How many NCAA National Championships has Duke won?

    A) 0
    B) 1
    C) 2
    D) 4

42) Since 1906, what is the only season Duke did not play basketball?

    A) 1914-15
    B) 1918-19
    C) 1944-45
    D) None of the above

43) Who was the Blue Devils' opponent in the first-ever game at Cameron Indoor Stadium?

    A) North Carolina
    B) Princeton
    C) Virginia
    D) Wake Forest

44) How many ACC Tournament championships has Duke won?

    A) 10
    B) 12
    C) 13
    D) 18

45) Who holds the career blocked shots record at Duke?

A) Mike Gminski
B) Sheldon Williams
C) Shane Battier
D) Christian Laettner

46) What year did Duke have two Consensus First Team All-Americans?

A) 1952
B) 1985
C) 2001
D) This has never happened

47) What is Duke's current non-conference home win streak?

A) 77 games
B) 89 games
C) 94 games
D) 102 games

48) Who holds Duke's record for most points scored in a single game?

A) Dick Groat
B) Danny Ferry
C) Jeff Mullins
D) J.J. Redick

49) Who holds Duke's career record for most points scored?

    A)   Christian Laettner
    B)   Johnny Dawkins
    C)   J.J. Redick
    D)   Mike Gminski

50) What year did Duke first celebrate a victory over North Carolina?

    A)   1920
    B)   1928
    C)   1935
    D)   1939

Duke has a proud student-athlete academic mission and track record. An impressive 91% of Duke's student athletes receive a degree. Twenty of the school's twenty-six varsity sports celebrate a 100% graduation rate in most years. Further, men's basketball players who complete four years of eligibility have a 97%-98% graduation rate. These are rather impressive figures when you consider that being on Coach K's basketball team at Duke is like a full-time job. A commitment to both academic and basketball excellence is a must to call yourself a Duke Blue Devil.

1) C – 1922-23 (The name was nominated and narrowly selected in 1921. Though it did not gain widespread usage until the following year when newspaper staff began using it to refer to the athletic teams.)

2) B – Royal Blue and White (Associated with the school's athletics since 1920, royal blue is also referred to as Duke Blue.)

3) B – Cameron Indoor Stadium (Originally known as Duke Indoor Stadium, it was renamed in honor of Coach Eddie Cameron on Jan. 22, 1972.)

4) A – 7 (Johnny Dawkins [1986], Danny Ferry [1989], Christian Laettner [1992], Elton Brand [1999], Shane Battier [2001], Jason Williams [2002], and J.J. Redick [2006])

5) B – "Fight! Blue Devils, Fight!" (Lyrics by Douglas Ballin and music by J.F. Hewitt)

6) D – Cameron Crazies (Around 1,200 seats are occupied at each home game by the Cameron Crazies.)

7) D – 15 (1963, 1964, 1966, 1978, 1986, 1988, 1989, 1990, 1991, 1992, 1994, 1999, 2001, 2004, and 2010)

8) A – Mike Krzyzewski (In his 30 years at Duke, Coach K has an overall record of 795-220.)

9) C – 1953 (Duke is a charter member of the ACC along with Clemson, Maryland, North Carolina, N.C. State, South Carolina, and Wake Forest.)

10) A – Pete Gaudet (Back problems required Coach K to take a leave from the team in 1995. Coach Gaudet led the Blue Devils to a 4-15 record in his absence.)

11) D – 1906 (Duke's first-ever game was played at home on March 2, 1906.)

12) D – 9,314 (A stadium renovation in 1987-88 expanded official seating capacity from 8,800.)

13) A – The Blue Devil (Named for WWI Alpine French soldiers known as "les Diables Bleus", who were distinguishable by their blue uniforms with capes.)

14) C – Bob Harris (Harris has been Duke's play-by-play sportscaster since Add Penfield's retirement in 1976. John Roth provides color commentary.)

15) A – The Ark (Built in 1898 by donations given to the school by Benjamin N. Duke. The intimate gymnasium could hold roughly 100 spectators.)

16) C – Davidson (Since 1909 the Blue Devils have played Davidson 104 times. Duke leads the series 87-17.)

17) B – No (Duke was defeated at home by Wake Forest 10-24 on March 2, 1906.)

18) A – Krzyzewskiville (The tent city can be populated with up to 1,200 Duke fans braving the elements for a coveted seat at a Blue Devils home game.)

19) D – Eddie Cameron (Coach Cameron led the Blue Devils from 1929-42.)

20) C – Ed Koffenberger (Koffenberger was Consensus Second Team All-American in 1947.)

21) B – No (In the 1905-06 season Duke was 2-3 overall.)

22) C – Boston College (Nov. 16, 1990 [Duke 100, BC 76])

23) D – Mike Krzyzewski (Coach K owns a 795-220 coaching record through 30 seasons at Duke.)

24) B – No. 3 (In the 18th week of the 2009-10 season the Blue Devils rose to No. 3 in the AP Poll.)

25) A – Bobby Hurley (On Feb. 24, 1993, Bobby had 16 assists versus Florida State [Duke 98, FSU 75].)

26) D – None of the above (Duke has never gone unbeaten through an entire season.)

27) A – 15 (The Blue Devils are currently in their longest streak for most consecutive NCAA Tournament appearances [1996-2010].)

28) B – False (Duke has only 2 one-loss seasons. In 1908-09 they were 8-1 and in 1911-12 they were 6-1 overall. Both teams were coached by W.W. Cap Card.)

29) A – Wake Forest (Duke has played the Demon
Deacons 234 times. N.C. State is a close second
with 233 all-time match ups.)

30) B – 3 (The Blue Devils were 2-3, 4-2, 2-3, 8-1, 4-4, and
4-3 respectively in their first six seasons.)

31) A – 29 (The most recent season this happened was in
2008-09 when Duke went 17-1 at home.)

32) D – Trinity Park (Duke's all-time first victory is recorded
as a 28-18 win over Trinity Park. The date of that
game is unrecorded.)

33) B – 18 (The 2009-10 season is the most recent season
in which Duke was undefeated at home.)

34) A – Johnny Dawkins (After 11 seasons as an assistant
coach at Duke, Dawkins was named head coach of
the Stanford Cardinal in April of 2008.)

35) B – 1940 (Known then as Duke Indoor Stadium, Duke
played its first game in the stadium on Jan. 6,
1940.)

36) A – True (The Blue Devils made 407 3-pointers in 39
games [10.44 per game] in the 2000-01 season.)

37) D – Ernie Beck (On Dec. 30, 1952, Beck scored 47
points against Duke [Duke 80, Pennsylvania 97].)

38) C – Football (Lyrics: "For the Touchdown's…")

39) A – 4 (N.C. State managed a victory over Duke with four field goals on March 8, 1968 [Duke 10, N.C. State 12].)

40) B – Motion (His free-flowing offense allows players to creatively take advantage of opportunities given to them by the defense.)

41) D – 4 (1991, 1992, 2001, and 2010)

42) D – None of the above (Including World War years, Duke has never missed a season of basketball.)

43) B – Princeton (On Jan. 6, 1940, Duke defeated Princeton 56-27 in the stadium's first game.)

44) D – 18 (1960, 1963, 1964, 1966, 1978, 1980, 1986, 1988, 1992, 1999, 2000, 2001, 2002, 2003, 2004, 2006, 2009, and 2010)

45) B – Sheldon Williams (From 2003-06, Williams accumulated 422 blocked shots in 139 games.)

46) C – 2001 (Shane Battier and Jason Williams)

47) A – 77 games (Duke's last loss to a non-conference opponent at home was to the St. John's Red Storm on Feb. 26, 2000 [Duke 82, St. John's 83].)

48) B – Danny Ferry (On Dec. 10, 1988, Ferry scored 58 points at Miami [Duke 117, Miami 102].)

49) C – J.J. Redick (From 2003-06 Redick scored 2,769 total career points for Duke.)

50) A – 1920 (On March 1, 1920, Duke celebrated its first all-time victory over North Carolina [19-18].)

Note: All answers valid as of the end of the 2009-10 season, unless otherwise indicated in the question itself.

1) For the decade of the 2000s, what ranking did Duke hold in the category of winningest team of the decade?

Answers begin on page 37

- A) First
- B) Second
- C) Third
- D) Fourth

2) What year was Duke's first overtime game?

- A) 1906
- B) 1909
- C) 1914
- D) 1920

3) All-time, how many Duke players have won ACC Rookie of the Year?

- A) 0
- B) 2
- C) 3
- D) 5

4) How many decades has Duke won at least 225 games?

- A) 2
- B) 3
- C) 5
- D) 7

5) What was the name of the first conference to which Duke belonged?

A) Southern Intercollegiate Athletic Association
B) Athletic Association of the Carolinas
C) Southern Conference
D) Southeastern Conference

6) How many consecutive seasons has Duke currently won 20 or more games?

A) 14
B) 16
C) 18
D) 20

7) Who holds the record for most rebounds against Duke in a single game?

A) Sean May, North Carolina
B) Clyde Lee, Vanderbilt
C) Len Chappell, Wake Forest
D) Lew Alcindor, UCLA

8) What is Duke's all-time largest margin of victory?

A) 50 points
B) 60 points
C) 70 points
D) 80 points

9) How many times has Duke beaten an AP No. 1 ranked team?

    A) 4
    B) 6
    C) 8
    D) 10

10) Has Duke ever lost to any of the U.S. Service Academies?

    A) Yes
    B) No

11) What is Duke's all-time winning percentage against North Carolina?

    A) .389
    B) .399
    C) .419
    D) .432

12) How many times has Duke won by 70 or more points?

    A) 2
    B) 4
    C) 5
    D) 7

13) How many triple-overtime games has Duke played?

    A) 1
    B) 3
    C) 5
    D) 7

14) Other than North Carolina, which ACC opponent has the most wins against the Blue Devils?

    A) Wake Forest
    B) N.C. State
    C) Maryland
    D) Virginia

15) What is the record for the most fouls by a Duke team in a single game?

    A) 25
    B) 30
    C) 35
    D) 40

16) What team handed Duke its all-time worst loss?

    A) Virginia
    B) Washington & Lee
    C) North Carolina
    D) West Virginia

17) To how many consecutive NCAA Tournaments has Mike Krzyzewski coached Duke?

    A) 9
    B) 11
    C) 15
    D) 18

18) What is Shane Battier's record at Duke for most charges taken in a career?

    A) 111
    B) 121
    C) 131
    D) 141

19) What is the longest winning streak for Duke in the Duke-North Carolina series?

    A) 3 games
    B) 5 games
    C) 7 games
    D) 8 games

20) Have the Blue Devils won 100 or more NCAA Tournament games?

    A) Yes
    B) No

21) Who was Duke's first-ever NCAA Tournament opponent?

    A) Villanova
    B) St. Joseph's
    C) NYU
    D) Loyola

22) How many total AP Top-10 finishes does Duke have?

    A) 18
    B) 22
    C) 26
    D) 30

23) How many times have Duke players been named to the All-NCAA Final Four Team?

    A) 19
    B) 25
    C) 29
    D) 33

24) Since 1955, what are the fewest points allowed by Duke in a single game?

    A) 0
    B) 2
    C) 8
    D) 12

25) Which of the following Blue Devils was only chosen once to the All-NCAA Final Four Team?

    A) Grant Hill
    B) Christian Laettner
    C) Trajan Langdon
    D) Bobby Hurley

26) What is the Blue Devils' largest halftime deficit in a game they went on to win?

    A) 29 points
    B) 33 points
    C) 37 points
    D) 41 points

27) What are the fewest points Duke has held North Carolina to in a single half?

    A) 0
    B) 3
    C) 6
    D) 11

28) Which Blue Devil holds the team record for most rebounds in a single game?

    A) Art Hayman
    B) Bernie Janicki
    C) Bob Lakata
    D) Mike Lewis

29) How many all-time Duke Basketball games have gone into overtime?

   A) 90
   B) 102
   C) 118
   D) 133

30) What is Duke's record for consecutive winning seasons?

   A) 11
   B) 14
   C) 17
   D) 22

31) How many Blue Devils have won ACC Player of the Year honors twice?

   A) 1
   B) 2
   C) 3
   D) 4

32) Who holds Duke's record for steals in a season?

   A) Jim Spanarkel
   B) Steve Wojciechowski
   C) Shane Battier
   D) Chris Duhon

33) What are the most three-pointers made in a single game by the Blue Devils?

    A) 9
    B) 12
    C) 14
    D) 18

34) How many times has Duke been in the Postseason NIT Tournament?

    A) 3
    B) 5
    C) 7
    D) None of the above

35) What is Duke's all-time largest loss to North Carolina?

    A) 24 points
    B) 32 points
    C) 36 points
    D) 42 points

36) How many times has Duke finished No.1 in the final AP Poll?

    A) 7
    B) 10
    C) 12
    D) 15

37) How many Postseason NIT Championships has Duke won?

    A) 1
    B) 3
    C) 5
    D) None of the above

38) Who is Duke's only three-time National Defensive Player of the Year?

    A) Grant Hill
    B) Shelden Williams
    C) Shane Battier
    D) Duke has only had two-time winners

39) How many times have Duke players won ACC Player of the Year?

    A) 13
    B) 16
    C) 19
    D) 22

40) Who holds Duke's single game free throws made record?

    A) Joe Belmont
    B) Bucky Allen
    C) Jim Spanarkel
    D) Dick Groat

41) What team broke Duke's 46-game home court winning streak in 2000?

    A) St. John's
    B) Wake Forest
    C) Maryland
    D) Clemson

42) What are the most three-pointers attempted in a single game by a Duke player?

    A) 11
    B) 12
    C) 15
    D) 18

43) Who holds Duke's career record for most games played?

    A) Christian Laettner
    B) Shane Battier
    C) Chris Duhon
    D) Greg Koubek

44) What are Duke's most consecutive ACC Regular Season titles?

    A) 2
    B) 3
    C) 5
    D) 7

45) Who was the Blue Devils' leading scorer in the 2009-10 season?

    A) Kyle Singler
    B) Jon Scheyer
    C) Nolan Smith
    D) Brian Zoubek

46) Other than the ACC, against which conference does Duke have the most wins?

    A) Atlantic 10
    B) Big East
    C) Southeastern
    D) Southern

47) Does Duke have an all-time winning record in overtime games?

    A) Yes
    B) No

48) Which conference has the most wins against Duke?

    A) Big East
    B) Big 10
    C) SEC
    D) Patriot League

49) What season did Duke win its first-ever ACC Regular Season title?

    A) 1954
    B) 1958
    C) 1963
    D) 1964

50) Who was Duke's opponent both times they appeared in the Jimmy V Classic?

    A) Purdue
    B) Kentucky
    C) Seton Hall
    D) UMass

The Blue Devils have appeared in 34 NCAA Tournaments since 1965. Rival North Carolina has appeared in 41. Surprisingly the two teams have never met in the tournament. In fact, the only time the two teams ever met in a post-season tournament was in the semifinals of the 1971 National Invitational Tournament. North Carolina would get a 73-69 victory in that game, leaving Duke to wait for its next opportunity to face the Tar Heels in NCAA or NIT tournament play.

1) A – First (Including the 1999-2000 season, Duke's 291 victories through the end of the 2008-09 season ranks Duke first amongst all Division I teams.)

2) C – 1914 (Although the year is known, Duke's first-ever overtime game and victory [33-25] was at home against N.C. State on an unrecorded date.)

3) D – 5 (Jim Spanarkel [1976], Mike Gminski [1977], Gene Banks [1978], Chris Duhon [2001], and Kyle Singler [2008])

4) B – 3 (1980s [226], 1990s [271], and 2000s [291])

5) C – Southern Conference (Duke became a member in the 1928-29 season.)

6) A – 14 (The streak started in 1996-97 [24-9] and continued through 2009-10 [35-5].)

7) B – Clyde Lee, Vanderbilt (On Dec. 11, 1963, Lee pulled down 26 rebounds at Vanderbilt [Duke 92, Vanderbilt 97].)

8) D – 80 points (In 1910 Duke defeated Furman by 80 points [Duke 85, Furman 5].)

9) C – 8 (All-time Duke is 8-21 versus AP No. 1-ranked teams.)

10) A – Yes (The Blue Devils are 1-0 versus Air Force, 9-3 versus Army, and 29-13 versus Navy.)

11) D – .432 (Duke's all-time record against North Carolina is 99-130.)

12) A – 2 (Duke defeated Furman by 80 points in 1910 and Harvard by 76 points in 1989.)

13) B – 3 (Feb. 24, 1982 [Duke 73, Clemson 72], March 2, 1968 [Duke 87, North Carolina 86], and Feb. 25, 1958 [Duke 68, Virginia 70])

14) B – N.C. State (The Blue Devils have a 136-97 all-time record versus the Wolfpack.)

15) D – 40 (This happened in a game versus Wake Forest on Jan. 12, 1954 [Duke 89, Wake Forest 96].)

16) B – Washington & Lee (In 1913 Washington & Lee defeated Duke by 75 points [15-90].)

17) C – 15 (This current streak began in 1996.)

18) A – 111 (He set the school record from 1998-2001.)

19) D – 8 games (From Feb. 23, 1951 to Feb. 20, 1954, Duke won eight straight games versus North Carolina.)

20) B – No (Through the 2010 tournament, Duke's all-time NCAA Tournament record is 94-30.)

21) A – Villanova (Duke faced Villanova in New York, N.Y. in 1955 [Duke 73, Villanova 74].)

22) D – 30 (Their first top-10 finish was No. 10 in 1958 and their most recent was No. 3 in 2010.)

23) B – 25 (Art Heyman was the first-ever in 1963 and John Scheyer and Nolan Smith were the most recent in 2010.)

24) D – 12 (On March 8, 1968, Duke held N.C. State to 12 total points, but still lost the game [Duke 10, N.C. State 12].)

25) C – Trajan Langdon (Trajan Langdon [1999], Grant Hill [1992 and 1994], Christian Laettner [1991 and 1992], and Bobby Hurley [1991 and 1992])

26) A – 29 points (Tulane led Duke 56-29 at halftime on Dec. 30, 1950. Duke fought back to win the game 74-72.)

27) A – 0 (On Feb. 24, 1979, Duke held the Tar Heels to zero points in the first half of play [Final score: Duke 47, North Carolina 40].)

28) B – Bernie Janicki (Janicki pulled down 31 total rebounds versus North Carolina on Feb. 29, 1952 [Duke 94, North Carolina 64].)

29) C – 118 (The first was in 1914 versus N.C. State and the most recent was on Feb. 7, 2009, versus Miami.)

30) D – 22 (Their longest-ever streak began in 1950-51 and lasted through 1971-72.)

31) B – 2 (Danny Ferry [1988 and 1989] and J.J. Redick [2005 and 2006])

32) A – Jim Spanarkel (In 1978 Spanarkel had 93 steals in 34 games for a 2.7 steals per game average.)

33) D – 18 (The Blue Devils have hit 18 3-point field goals on three occasions: versus N.C. AT&T on Dec. 30, 2000, versus Monmouth on March 15, 2001, and versus Radford on Nov. 21, 2009.)

34) B – 5 (1967, 1968, 1970, 1971, and 1981)

35) C – 36 points (On March 5, 1921, Duke lost by a final score of 19-55 to North Carolina.)

36) A – 7 (1986, 1992, 1999, 2000, 2001, 2002, and 2006)

37) D – None of the above (Duke's highest finish in the Postseason NIT was fourth in 1971.)

38) C – Shane Battier (1999, 2000, and 2001)

39) A – 13 (The first was Art Heyman in 1963 and the most recent was J.J. Redick in 2006.)

40) B – Bucky Allen (Allen hit 20 of 23 free throws versus N.C. State on Jan. 5, 1957.)

41) C – Maryland (The steak ended with an 87-98 loss to Maryland on Feb. 9, 2000.)

42) D – 18 (Bobby Hurley attempted 18 three-pointers versus Cal on March 20, 1993 [Duke 77, Cal 82].)

43) A – Christian Laettner (From 1989-92 Laettner played in 148 games at Duke.)

44) C – 5 (From 1997-2001 Duke won the ACC Regular Season Championship.)

45) B – Jon Scheyer (Scheyer led all Blue Devil scorers with 728 points in 2009-10, for a 18.2 points-per-game average.)

46) D – Southern (Duke has an all-time record of 140-24 versus Southern Conference teams.)

47) A – Yes (The Blue Devils are 65-53 [.551] in overtime games.)

48) C – SEC (Duke holds a 113-58 all-time record versus SEC schools.)

49) A – 1954 (Duke secured its first-ever ACC title with a 9-1 conference record in 1954.)

50) B – Kentucky (Duke faced Kentucky in the Jimmy V Classic Men's Basketball Tournament on Dec. 18, 2001 [Duke 95, Kentucky 92OT] and on Dec. 22, 1998 [Duke 71, Kentucky 60].)

Note: All answers valid as of the end of the 2009-10 season, unless otherwise indicated in the question itself.

1) How many times has Duke appeared in the NCAA Tournament Championship game?

Answers begin on page 56

    A) 6
    B) 7
    C) 10
    D) 12

2) When was the first-ever 20-win season at Duke?

    A) 1910-11
    B) 1916-17
    C) 1923-24
    D) 1935-36

3) What is the Blue Devils' record for consecutive ACC losses?

    A) 5
    B) 7
    C) 8
    D) 9

4) What year was the first-ever game between Duke and North Carolina?

    A) 1914
    B) 1916
    C) 1918
    D) 1920

5) What are the most losses in one season by Duke at Cameron Indoor Stadium?

    A) 8
    B) 9
    C) 13
    D) 14

6) What is Duke's all-time record for consecutive winning seasons?

    A) 13
    B) 18
    C) 19
    D) 22

7) Who is the only Blue Devil to lead the team in scoring for four consecutive years?

    A) Art Heyman
    B) Danny Ferry
    C) Johnny Dawkins
    D) J.J. Redick

8) Has Duke won greater than 90 of its all-time home openers?

    A) Yes
    B) No

9) What are the fewest Duke players to foul out in a season?

    A) 5
    B) 15
    C) 25
    D) 35

10) When was the first-ever 30-win season at Duke?

    A) 1977-78
    B) 1979-80
    C) 1985-86
    D) 1987-88

11) Who holds Duke's record for steals in a career?

    A) Chris Duhon
    B) Grant Hill
    C) Tommy Amaker
    D) Shane Battier

12) What are the most points an opposing player scored on Duke in the 2009-10 season?

    A) 20
    B) 22
    C) 24
    D) 26

13) Where did Eddie Cameron coach immediately before Duke?

    A) North Carolina
    B) Washington & Lee
    C) N.C. State
    D) Wake Forest

14) Has Duke ever had a player drafted No. 1 overall in the NBA Draft?

    A) Yes
    B) No

15) Which medal did the Krzyzewski-led "Redeem Team" win at the 2008 Beijing Olympics?

    A) None
    B) Bronze
    C) Silver
    D) Gold

16) What is Duke's largest-ever margin of victory against North Carolina?

    A) 31 points
    B) 33 points
    C) 35 points
    D) 37 points

17) What was the height of the tallest player on the Blue Devils' 2009-10 roster?

    A) 6'11"
    B) 7'1"
    C) 7'3"
    D) 7'4"

18) In the Duke Alma Mater, which of the following is named?

    A) Sea
    B) Ocean
    C) Lake
    D) River

19) What country is former Duke guard Martynas Pocius from?

    A) Latvia
    B) Slovenia
    C) Czech Republic
    D) Lithuania

20) Was Steve Wojciechowski ever a team captain at Duke?

    A) Yes
    B) No

21) What was the last regular-season non-conference loss for the Blue Devils in 2009-10?

    A) Wisconsin
    B) Tulsa
    C) Georgetown
    D) None of the above

22) Who was Duke's first-ever official basketball coach?

    A) Joseph E. Brinn
    B) W.W. Cap Card
    C) Noble L. Clay
    D) Bob Doak

23) How many seasons has Duke made the NCAA Tournament?

    A) 28
    B) 30
    C) 34
    D) 38

24) What is the all-time largest deficit Duke has overcome to win a game?

    A) 32 points
    B) 33 points
    C) 37 points
    D) 38 points

25) Did Duke play in the first-ever nationally televised regular-season college basketball game?

    A) Yes
    B) No

26) Which of these seasons did Duke lead the nation in three-point field goal attempts?

    A) 1991-92
    B) 1997-98
    C) 2000-01
    D) 2005-06

27) What are the most consecutive ACC Tournament Championships Duke has won?

    A) 4
    B) 5
    C) 7
    D) 8

28) Who was the first-ever African-American to play for the Blue Devils?

    A) Billy Jones
    B) Julius "Pete" Johnson
    C) William Garrett
    D) Claudius "C.B." Claiborne

29) Which decade were Duke players named consensus
First Team All-American the greatest number of times?

    A) 1960s
    B) 1980s
    C) 1990s
    D) 2000s

30) How many undefeated seasons did Duke have on their
home court at "The Ark"?

    A) 0
    B) 1
    C) 2
    D) 3

31) What was the construction cost of Duke Indoor
Stadium?

    A) $250,000
    B) $300,000
    C) $400,000
    D) $450,000

32) What are the most points ever scored in one half by
Duke?

    A) 49
    B) 50
    C) 61
    D) 72

33) What category did Duke lead the nation in 1989-90?

A) Most Free Throws Made
B) Fewest Personal Fouls
C) Most Points
D) None of the above

34) Since 1969, who is the only Blue Devil player to lead the team in assists for four consecutive seasons?

A) Dick DeVenzio
B) Jim Spanarkel
C) Bobby Hurley
D) Chris Duhon

35) What are the most consecutive ACC Tournament Championship games Duke has lost?

A) Never lost consecutive games
B) 2
C) 3
D) 4

36) What are the most consecutive NCAA Tournament losses Duke has had?

A) Never lost consecutive games
B) 2
C) 3
D) 4

37) How many times has Duke appeared in the ACC Tournament Championship game?

A) 21
B) 23
C) 29
D) 35

38) Which team gave Duke its first-ever home loss at Cameron Indoor Stadium?

A) North Carolina
B) Davidson
C) Pennsylvania
D) The Citadel

39) Which ACC school has the highest winning percentage against the Blue Devils?

A) N.C. State
B) Maryland
C) Georgia Tech
D) North Carolina

40) Against which team does Duke have the most 100-point games?

A) Maryland
B) Virginia
C) Davidson
D) Harvard

41) What are the most consecutive NCAA Tournament games that Duke has won?

    A) 9
    B) 11
    C) 13
    D) 15

42) Who was the first Blue Devil to appear on the cover of *Sports Illustrated*?

    A) Jeff Mullins
    B) Gene Banks
    C) Art Hayman
    D) Dick Groat

43) Does Coach K hold a Midnight Madness practice to open every Duke basketball season?

    A) Yes
    B) No

44) Who is the only Blue Devil to be named All-National Invitational Tournament?

    A) Mark Alarie
    B) Jack Marin
    C) Randy Denton
    D) Billy McCaffrey

45) Who was Duke's first-ever ACC opponent?

   A) Virginia
   B) Wake Forest
   C) South Carolina
   D) N.C. State

46) In 1988 how many additional student seats were added to Cameron Indoor Stadium?

   A) 550
   B) 650
   C) 750
   D) 850

47) Which Blue Devil played in the most NCAA Tournament games?

   A) Greg Koubek
   B) Christian Laettner
   C) Thomas Hill
   D) Antonio Lang

48) Each of Duke's National Championship teams also won the ACC regular season and conference tournament.

   A) True
   B) False

49) How many times has Duke been invited to the White House to receive honors from the President?

   A) 0
   B) 1
   C) 2
   D) 4

50) What is Duke's record for most consecutive ACC wins?

   A) 31 games
   B) 34 games
   C) 37 games
   D) 40 games

We have all used the term at one time or another. "Air ball! Air ball!", we shout playfully or tauntingly at someone. Before they were known as the Cameron Crazies, Duke's sixth man, the student section, loved to disrupt opposing teams. In a game versus North Carolina in 1979 fans erupted in a chant of air ball when a Tar Heel completely missed a shot. To this day fans around the world never miss an opportunity to let an opponent know when they have shot the dreaded air ball.

1) C – 10 (1964, 1978, 1986, 1990, 1991, 1992, 1994, 1999, 2001, and 2010)

2) B – 1916-17 (The Blue Devils went 20-4 under Coach Chick Doak that season to earn their first 20-win season.)

3) D – 9 (From Jan. 4, 1995 to Feb. 4, 1995, Duke lost nine consecutive games to ACC opponents.)

4) D – 1920 (Jan. 24, 1920, marked the beginning of the Blue Devils-Tar Heels rivalry. North Carolina defeated Duke 25-36 at North Carolina.)

5) A – 8 (The 1943-44 season saw Duke lose eight games at home under Coach Gerry Gerard.)

6) D – 22 (From 1950-51 to 1971-72 Duke had 22 consecutive winning seasons under Coaches Bradley, Bubas, and Waters.)

7) C – Johnny Dawkins (Many players led the team for three seasons, but Dawkins is the only one to lead it for four [1983-86].)

8) B – No (Duke's all-time record in home openers is 81-24.)

9) A – 5 (In both the 1961-62 and 1993-94 seasons Duke only had five players foul out of games the entire seasons.)

10) C – 1985-86 (A 37-3 record helped Duke eclipse the 30-win mark for the first time in its storied history.)

11) A – Chris Duhon (From 2001-04 Duhon had 301 steals in 144 games [2.1 steals per game].)

12) D – 26 (Wisconsin's Trevon Hughes scored 26 points versus Duke in 2009-10.)

13) B – Washington & Lee (At age 23 Coach Cameron spent one year as assistant football coach at W&L.)

14) A – Yes (Art Heyman was drafted No. 1 overall by New York in 1963 and Elton Brand No. 1 overall by Chicago in 1999.)

15) D – Gold (Coach K led the U.S. Men's Basketball Team to a 118-107 victory over Spain in the Gold Medal Game.)

16) C – 35 points (In a game played on Feb. 29, 1964, at North Carolina, Duke won in a score of 104-69.)

17) B – 7'1" (Brian Zoubek was officially listed at 7'1".)

18) A – Sea (Lyrics: "…And though on life's broad sea…")

19) D – Lithuania (His home town is Vilnius, Lithuania.)

20) A – Yes (Current Assistant Coach Wojciechowski was a team captain along with teammates Trajan Langdon and Roshown McLeod in 1997-98.)

21) C – Georgetown (Duke was defeated by Georgetown 77-89 on Jan. 30, 2010, at Washington, D.C.)

22) B – W.W. Cap Card (Coach Card led Duke, known then as Trinity College, from 1905-06 through 1911-12.)

23) C – 34 (1955, 1960, 1963, 1964, 1966, 1978, 1979, 1980, 1984, 1985, 1986, 1987, 1988, 1989, 1990, 1991, 1992, 1993, 1994, 1996, 1997, 1998, 1999, 2000, 2001, 2002, 2003, 2004, 2005, 2006, 2007, 2008, 2009, and 2010)

24) A – 32 points (The Blue Devils trailed Tulane 22-54 in the first half of a game played on Dec. 30, 1950 [Final score: Duke 74, Tulane 72].)

25) B – No (UCLA and Houston played the first televised college basketball game on Jan. 20, 1968.)

26) C – 2000-01 (The Blue Devils set an NCAA record that season with 1,057 3-point field goal attempts.)

27) B – 5 (From 1999-2003 Duke won five consecutive ACC Tournament Championships.)

28) D – Claudius "C.B." Claiborne (Claiborne was Duke's first African-American athlete. He played for Duke from 1966-67 to 1968-69.)

29) D – 2000s (Four Blue Devils have been named Consensus First Team All-American on five occasions through 2007-08: Chris Carrawell [2000], Shane Battier [2001], Jason Williams [2001 and 2002], and J.J. Redick [2005].)

30) A – 0 (The fewest losses Duke ever had in a single season at "The Ark" was one [8-1 in 1908-09 and 6-1 in 1911-12].)

31) C – $400,000 (Construction on the stadium was completed in 1940.)

32) D – 72 (The Blue Devils have scored 72 in a half twice, once versus Virginia on Feb. 11, 1965, and once versus Harvard on Nov. 25, 1989.)

33) A – Most Free Throws Made (In fact, they set a current NCAA record with 888 free throws made.)

34) C – Bobby Hurley (From 1990-93 Bobby had 288, 289, 237, and 262 assists each season respectively.)

35) A – Never lost consecutive games (Duke has never lost two or more consecutive ACC Championship games.)

36) B – 2 (On four occasions since 1955 Duke has lost two consecutive NCAA Tournament games. Due to the single-elimination format of the tournament, those losses spanned two seasons.)

37) C – 29 (Their first appearance was in 1955 and their most recent was in 2010.)

38) A – North Carolina (On Feb. 22, 1940, North Carolina handed Duke its first-ever loss [27-31] in the new Duke Indoor Stadium [renamed Cameron Indoor Stadium in 1972].)

39) D – North Carolina (Having won 130 of 229 games, the Tar Heels have a .567 all-time winning percentage against the Blue Devils.)

40) B – Virginia (The Blue Devils have scored 100 or more points on the Cavaliers 18 times. The most recent was a 104-93 victory on Jan. 15, 2003.)

41) C – 13 (This includes six in the 1991, six in the 1992, and one in the 1993 tournaments.)

42) A – Jeff Mullins (Although he was not featured, Mullins appeared on the cover with UCLA's Walt Hazzard in 1964. Gene Banks would be the first Duke basketball player to be featured in 1978.)

43) B – No (Midnight practice is no longer a regular event. The Blue-White game now showcases the team for the upcoming season during Countdown to Craziness.)

44) C – Randy Denton (1971)

45) A – Virginia (Jan. 2, 1954 [Duke 86, Virginia 64].)

46) C – 750 (This expansion increased capacity to 9,314, its current level.)

47) B – Christian Laettner (He appeared in 23 NCAA Tournament games from 1989-92.)

48) B – False (The 1990-01 team failed to win the ACC Tournament Championship game vs. North Carolina [Duke 74, North Carolina 96].)

49) D – 4 (Once after each National Championship: 1991, 1992, 2001, and 2010)

50) A – 31 games (From Feb. 8, 1998 to Feb. 9, 2000)

Note: All answers valid as of the end of the 2009-10 season, unless otherwise indicated in the question itself.

1) Which of these schools has Duke never beaten?

Answers begin on page 75

    A)   LaSalle
    B)   Texas
    C)   Stanford
    D)   Portland

2) Which of these games set Duke's all-time attendance record?

    A)   West Virginia 2010
    B)   Kansas 1991
    C)   Arizona 2001
    D)   Kentucky 1998

3) From 1997 to 2007 how many consecutive polls was Duke ranked in the top 25 of the AP Poll?

    A)   180
    B)   200
    C)   220
    D)   240

4) What was Duke's all-time lowest seeding in the NCAA Tournament?

    A)   No. 4
    B)   No. 5
    C)   No. 7
    D)   No. 8

5) How many schools have produced more National Association of Basketball Coaches National Defensive Player of the Year recipients than Duke?

    A) 0
    B) 1
    C) 3
    D) 4

6) Which Blue Devil led the team in dunks from 1987-90?

    A) Alaa Abdelnaby
    B) Mark Alarie
    C) Robert Brickey
    D) None of the above

7) Prior to 2008, when was the last year Wake Forest defeated the Blue Devils in basketball?

    A) 2003
    B) 2005
    C) 2006
    D) 2007

8) Who holds the record for the most points scored in a freshman year at Duke?

    A) Elton Brand
    B) Jim Spanarkel
    C) J.J. Redick
    D) Gene Banks

9) How many times has Duke beaten North Carolina at the Dean E. Smith Center?

    A) 7
    B) 9
    C) 11
    D) 12

10) Who holds Duke's record for most minutes played in a single game?

    A) John Frye
    B) Dick DeVenzio
    C) Chip Engelland
    D) Howard Hurt

11) Which of the following Duke players scored 40 or more points in an NCAA Tournament game?

    A) Jeff Mullins
    B) Bobby Hurley
    C) Jason Williams
    D) Danny Ferry

12) Where was the first-ever Duke game held?

    A) Trinity Men's Gym
    B) Angier B. Duke Gymnasium
    C) W. W. Card Arena
    D) Durham HS Gym

13) How many times has a Coach K-led Duke team been beaten while ranked No. 1 in the AP Poll?

    A) 16 games
    B) 19 games
    C) 24 games
    D) 26 games

14) Which one-season or less Duke head coach had the highest winning percentage?

    A) Neill McGeachy
    B) James Baldwin
    C) Joseph E. Brinn
    D) Walter J. Rothensies

15) Which of these Blue Devils had the most double-digit scoring games in their college career?

    A) J.J. Redick
    B) Johnny Dawkins
    C) Mark Alarie
    D) Christian Laettner

16) How many games did it take Mike Krzyzewski to get to 500 victories at Duke?

    A) 660
    B) 670
    C) 680
    D) 690

17) The 1991-92 Blue Devils were ranked No. 1 in the AP Poll throughout the entire season.

    A) True
    B) False

18) How many total weeks has Duke held No. 1 in the AP Poll?

    A) 100
    B) 105
    C) 111
    D) 115

19) How many seasons have the Blue Devils played in the Maui Invitational?

    A) 2
    B) 4
    C) 6
    D) 8

20) How many Duke head coaches coached one season or less?

    A) 5
    B) 6
    C) 7
    D) 8

21) Did the Blue Devils play 10 or more games in any season coached by W.W. Cap Card?

A) Yes
B) No

22) Including home, road, and neutral site games since 1970, how many times has Duke led the nation in attendance?

A) 0
B) 1
C) 4
D) 5

23) How many games has Duke played in when they and their opponent were both ranked in the top two of the AP Poll?

A) 2
B) 4
C) 6
D) 8

24) Which school have the Blue Devils never played?

A) Case Western Reserve
B) Radford
C) Toledo
D) Butler

25) Which season did Duke score the most total points?

    A) 1985-86
    B) 1990-91
    C) 1991-92
    D) 1998-99

26) Has Duke passed the 2,000-win milestone?

    A) Yes
    B) No

27) How many times has Duke been a No. 1 seed in the NCAA Tournament?

    A) 8
    B) 9
    C) 11
    D) 13

28) Where did Vic Bubas coach before Duke?

    A) George Mason
    B) Wake Forest
    C) North Carolina
    D) N.C. State

29) What decade did Duke have its lowest winning percentage?

    A) 1920s
    B) 1930s
    C) 1940s
    D) 1950s

30) Who was the first-ever team captain for the Blue Devils?

    A) Bill Lilly
    B) Thad G. Stem
    C) Emsley Armfield
    D) Paul Kiker

31) How many Blue Devils have scored 1,000+ career points?

    A) 41
    B) 45
    C) 51
    D) 60

32) Which team's players have scored the most points against Duke at Cameron Indoor Stadium?

    A) Wake Forest
    B) North Carolina
    C) N.C. State
    D) Maryland

33) What was the largest-ever margin of victory for the Blue Devils in an NCAA Tournament game?

    A) 41 points
    B) 43 points
    C) 47 points
    D) 49 points

34) Duke's final game of the 2009-10 season was played in which city?

    A) Indianapolis, Ind.
    B) Charlotte, N.C.
    C) Tampa Bay, Fla.
    D) Anaheim, Calif.

35) Which of the following players did not score over 2,000 career points while at Duke?

    A) Mark Alarie
    B) Mike Gminski
    C) Jim Spanarkel
    D) Trajan Langdon

36) Duke has had four players drafted in the same year in the NBA Draft on two separate occasions.

    A) True
    B) False

37) Who was the most recent player to lead Duke in scoring for three seasons?

   A)   Jason Williams
   B)   Danny Ferry
   C)   J.J. Redick
   D)   Christian Laettner

38) How many jersey numbers has Duke retired?

   A)   11
   B)   13
   C)   15
   D)   17

39) What is Duke's all-time highest winning percentage in a two-year period?

   A)   .920
   B)   .933
   C)   .956
   D)   None of the above

40) What are Duke's most consecutive victories to open a season?

   A)   12
   B)   14
   C)   15
   D)   17

41) Duke holds the NCAA Division I record for most victories over a four-year period.

    A) True
    B) False

42) What was Duke's biggest jump ever from not ranked the previous week to ranked in the AP Poll?

    A) No. 6
    B) No. 9
    C) No. 12
    D) No. 15

43) Which team gave Duke its largest-ever defeat in the NCAA Tournament?

    A) UCLA
    B) Kentucky
    C) Indiana
    D) UNLV

44) What is Duke's record for most losses in a season at Cameron Indoor Stadium?

    A) 7 games
    B) 8 games
    C) 9 games
    D) 10 games

45) Prior to 2008, who was the only Duke player to be awarded ACC Defensive Player of the Year?

   A) Shelden Williams
   B) Shane Battier
   C) Tommy Amaker
   D) Steve Wojciechowski

46) Where did former Duke head coach Bucky Waters play college basketball?

   A) Wake Forest
   B) Virginia
   C) N.C. State
   D) Duke

47) Did Blue Devils' legend Art Heyman originally commit to North Carolina before signing with Duke?

   A) Yes
   B) No

48) How many seasons has Duke gone undefeated at Cameron Indoor Stadium?

   A) 13
   B) 15
   C) 17
   D) 18

49) How many Blue Devils have played for the U.S. Men's Olympic basketball team?

    A) 2
    B) 3
    C) 4
    D) 5

50) What is Duke's all-time record in the ACC/Big Ten Challenge?

    A) 6-3
    B) 7-2
    C) 8-1
    D) None of the above

Sustainable programs rely heavily on their ability to recruit the nation's top talent out of high school. Duke has proven to be exceptionally adept at doing precisely that. Of the most coveted high school stars are the McDonald's All-Americans. In 2008-09 approximately 36 teams put a McDonald's All-American on the hardwood. Duke itself played seven. Greg Paulus earned this honor in 2005; Jon Scheyer, Gerald Henderson, and Lance Thomas in 2006; Kyle Singler and Nolan Smith in 2007; and Elliot Williams in 2008. Although having this depth in McDonalds's All-Americans does not ensure success, it certainly does not hurt.

1) C – Stanford (Duke is 0-2 all-time versus the Stanford Cardinal.)

2) A – West Virginia 2010 (Officially 71,298 fans attended this game in 2010, which exceeded the National Finals game attendance of 70,930.)

3) B – 200 (This streak is the second longest in AP Poll history.)

4) D – No. 8 (In 1996 Duke was the No. 8 seed in the Southeast Regional.)

5) A – 0 (Duke players won the award nine times. Connecticut is second with four recipients.)

6) C – Robert Brickey (He had 17 in 1987, 34 in 1988, 56 in 1989, and 40 in 1990 to lead all Duke dunkers.)

7) B – 2005 (On Feb. 2, 2005, Wake Forest defeated Duke [92-89] in Winston-Salem.)

8) D – Gene Banks (In 1978 Banks scored 581 points as a freshman.)

9) C – 11 (This includes Duke's Feb. 10, 2010, 64-54 victory in Chapel Hill.)

10) D – Howard Hurt (In a game versus Dayton on Dec. 30, 1959, Hurt played 55 minutes.)

11) A – Jeff Mullins (On March 13, 1964, Mullins scored 43 points versus Villanova.)

12) B – Angier B. Duke Gymnasium (Also known as The Ark, it was located on Trinity College's campus.)

13) C – 24 games (Coach K's Blue Devils are 166-24 [.874] while ranked No. 1 in the AP Poll.)

14) D – Walter J. Rothensies (Coach Rothensies led Duke to a one-year record of 10-4 [.714] in 1920.)

15) B – Johnny Dawkins (From 1983-86 Dawkins recorded 129 games with double-digit scoring.)

16) A – 660 (Duke defeated Villanova [98-85] on Nov. 17, 2000, to earn Coach K his 500th victory at Duke.)

17) A – True (Only 12 programs have ever done this.)

18) C – 111 (More than all other ACC members combined.)

19) B – 4 (1992-93 [3-0], 1997-98 [3-0], 2001-02 [3-0], and 2007-08 [3-0])

20) D – 8 (Joseph E. Brinn [1913], Bob Doak [1916], Henry P. Cole [1919], Walter J. Rothensies [1920], Floyd Egan [1921], James Baldwin [1922], Neill McGeachy [1974], and interim coach Pete Gaudet [1995])

21) B – No (The most games played in any season under W.W. Cap Card were 9. It was the 1908-09 season in which Duke went 8-1.)

22) B – 1 (In 2001 Duke led the league with 650,550 total attendance in all 39 games played.)

23) C – 6 (Duke is 3-3 in "No. 1 vs. No. 2" games.)

24) A – Case Western Reserve (Duke is 2-0 versus Butler, 2-0 versus Radford, and 1-0 versus Toledo.)

25) D – 1998-99 (Duke scored 3,581 points in 39 games that season to set the team and an ACC record.)

26) B – No (Duke has won 1,912 games in its history.)

27) C – 11 (1986, 1992, 1998, 1999, 2000, 2001, 2002, 2004, 2005, 2006, and 2010)

28) D – N.C. State (Coach Bubas was an assistant coach for the Wolfpack from 1951-59.)

29) A – 1920s (1920s [.548], 1930s [.682], 1940s [.681], and 1950s [.661])

30) B – Thad G. Stem (Stem was team captain in both 1905-06 and 1906-07.)

31) D – 60 (J.J. Redick's 2,769 career points leads all Blue Devils. The most recent player to join the 1,000-point club was Nolan Smith with 1,147 career points through 2009-10.)

32) A – Wake Forest (The Demon Deacons' Dickie Hemric scored 2 70 career points in 9 games from 1954-57 versus Duke at Cameron Indoor Stadium. Later Len Chappell would score 255 points in 10 games from 1960-63 in the stadium.)

33) C – 47 points (Duke defeated two tournament opponents by 47 points: UConn 101-54 on March 14, 1964 and Winthrop 84-37 on March 14, 2002.)

34) A – Indianapolis, Ind. (Duke's final game of the 2009-10 season came in the National Finals of the NCAA Tournament versus Butler [Duke 61, Butler 59] played at Lucas Oil Stadium.)

35) D – Trajan Langdon (Langdon had 1,974 career points at Duke. Duke's 2,000-point scorers include: J.J. Redick 2,769, Johnny Dawkins 2,556, Christian Laettner 2,460, Mike Gminski 2,323, Danny Ferry 2,155, Mark Alarie 2,136, Gene Banks 2,079, Jason Williams 2,079, and Jim Spanarkel 2,012.)

36) A – True (In 1986 Johnny Dawkins, Mark Alarie, David Henderson, and Jay Bilas were all drafted. Then in 1999 Elton Brand, Trajan Langdon, Corey Maggette, and William Avery were all drafted.)

37) C – J.J. Redick (589 points in 2004, 721 points in 2005, and 964 points in 2006)

38) B – 13 (Number, name, and year retired: #10 Dick Groat 1952, #43 Mike Gminski 1980, #24 Johnny Dawkins 1986, #35 Danny Ferry 1989, #25 Art Heyman 1990, #32 Christian Laettner 1992, #11 Bobby Hurley 1993, #33 Grant Hill 1994, #44 Jeff Mullins 1994, #31 Shane Battier 2001, #22 Jason Williams 2003, #23 Shelden Williams 2007, and #4 J.J. Redick 2007)

39) A – .920 (Duke had a combined winning percentage of .920 [69-6] in 1998-99.)

40) D – 17 (In both the 1991-92 and 2005-06 seasons Duke opened with 17 consecutive wins.)

41) A – True (From 1998-2001 the Blue Devils were 133-15. Duke is also second in this category with a 132-15 record from 1999-2002.)

42) C – No. 12 (On Nov. 27, 1995, Duke jumped to No. 12 from being unranked [not in the top 25] in the AP Poll the previous week.)

43) D – UNLV (On March 2, 1990, UNLV handed Duke a 30-point loss [103-73] in the NCAA Tournament Championship game.)

44) B – 8 games (Duke lost 8 home games in 1933-34.)

45) A – Shelden Williams (Williams received the honor in 2005 and 2006.)

46) C – N.C. State (Waters played for Coach Everett Case in the 1950s.)

47) A – Yes (Heyman caused controversy after he committed to North Carolina's Frank McGuire then changed his mind to attend Duke.)

48) B – 15 (1941-42 [11-0], 1957-58 [9-0], 1960-61 [8-0], 1962-63 [11-0], 1963-64 [10-0], 1965-66 [10-0], 1977-78 [12-0], 1985-86 [15-0], 1990-91 [16-0], 1991-92 [13-0], 1997-98 [15-0], 1998-99 [14-0], 2001-02 [13-0], 2002-03 [15-0], and 2009-10 [17-0])

49) D – 5 (Jeff Mullins [1964], Tate Armstrong [1976], Christian Laettner [1992], Grant Hill [1996], and Carlos Boozer [2004 and 2008])

50) C – 8-1 (Duke has only one loss in an ACC/Big Ten Challenge. In 1999-00 they defeated Illinois [72-69], in 2000-01 Illinois [78-77], in 2001-02 Iowa [80-62], in 2002-03 Ohio State [91-76], in 2003-04 Michigan State [72-50], in 2004-05 Michigan State [81-75], in 2007-08 Wisconsin [82-58], and in 2008-09 Purdue [76-60]. Their only loss came at Wisconsin [69-73] in 2009-10.)

Note: All answers valid as of the end of the 2009-10 season, unless otherwise indicated in the question itself.

1) Where did Coach K coach immediately before Duke?

Answers begin on page 83

    A)   Indiana
    B)   Navy
    C)   Illinois
    D)   Army

2) How many times has Duke begun the season ranked No. 1 in the first AP Poll?

    A)   4
    B)   5
    C)   6
    D)   7

3) How many 30-win seasons has Mike Krzyzewski had at Duke?

    A)   9
    B)   11
    C)   13
    D)   14

4) How many Duke players have been drafted in the NBA Draft?

    A)   50
    B)   61
    C)   73
    D)   83

5) What is the record for most 100-point games by opponents at Cameron Indoor Stadium in a season?

    A) 3
    B) 4
    C) 5
    D) 6

6) How many Duke players have won an Olympic gold medal?

    A) 2
    B) 3
    C) 4
    D) 5

7) Which Blue Devil is tied with J.J. Redick for most points scored in an ACC Tournament game?

    A) Bob Verga
    B) Jason Williams
    C) Daniel Ewing
    D) Danny Ferry

8) How many Duke players have been drafted in the first round of the NBA Draft?

    A) 25
    B) 26
    C) 29
    D) 31

9) How many Blue Devils have been named CoSIDA Academic All-American?

    A) 5
    B) 6
    C) 9
    D) 10

10) How many times did Duke trail at halftime in an NCAA Championship game they went on to win?

    A) 0
    B) 1
    C) 2
    D) 3

1) D – Army (Coach K led Army from 1975-80 [73-59].)
2) C – 6 (1979, 1989, 1992, 1999, 2002, and 2006)
3) B – 11 (1985-86 [37-3], 1990-91 [32-7], 1991-92 [34-2], 1997-98 [32-4], 1998-99 [37-2], 2000-01 [35-4], 2001-02 [31-4], 2003-04 [31-6], 2005-06 [32-4], 2008-09 [30-7], and 2009-10 [35-5])
4) C – 73 (Dike Groat was the first in 1952 [No. 3 overall by Detroit] and Gerald Henderson was the most recent [No. 12 overall by Charlotte] in 2009.)
5) A – 3 (1982-83: Duke 91, Virginia 104; Duke 90, Maryland 101; and Duke 81, North Carolina 105)
6) D – 5 (Jeff Mullins, Tate Armstrong, Christian Laettner, Grant Hill, and Carlos Boozer)
7) A – Bob Verga (Verga scored 35 points against Virginia on March 19, 1967. Redick scored 35 points versus N.C. State on March 12, 2005.)
8) C – 29 (Ranging from Dick Groat [Pistons] in 1952 to Gerald Henderson [Charlotte] in 2009.)
9) D – 10 (Paulus, Battier, Buckley, DeVenzio, Dunleavy, Fleischer, Gminski, Melchionni, Snyder, and Spanarkel)
10) B – 1 (In 1992 Michigan led Duke 31-30 at the half.)

Note: All answers valid as of the end of the 2009-10 season, unless otherwise indicated in the question itself.

Player / Team Score Sheet

Name:_____

Preseason			Regular Season			Conference Tournament			Championship Game			Overtime Bonus	
1	26		1	26		1	26		1	26		1	
2	27		2	27		2	27		2	27		2	
3	28		3	28		3	28		3	28		3	
4	29		4	29		4	29		4	29		4	
5	30		5	30		5	30		5	30		5	
6	31		6	31		6	31		6	31		6	
7	32		7	32		7	32		7	32		7	
8	33		8	33		8	33		8	33		8	
9	34		9	34		9	34		9	34		9	
10	35		10	35		10	35		10	35		10	
11	36		11	36		11	36		11	36			
12	37		12	37		12	37		12	37			
13	38		13	38		13	38		13	38			
14	39		14	39		14	39		14	39			
15	40		15	40		15	40		15	40			
16	41		16	41		16	41		16	41			
17	42		17	42		17	42		17	42			
18	43		18	43		18	43		18	43			
19	44		19	44		19	44		19	44			
20	45		20	45		20	45		20	45			
21	46		21	46		21	46		21	46			
22	47		22	47		22	47		22	47			
23	48		23	48		23	48		23	48			
24	49		24	49		24	49		24	49			
25	50		25	50		25	50		25	50			

____x 1 =____ ____x 2 =____ ____x 3 =____ ____x 4 =____ ____x 4 =____

Multiply total number correct by point value/quarter to calculate totals for each quarter.

Add total of all quarters below.

Total Points:_____

Thank you for playing *Blue Devilology Trivia Challenge*.

Additional score sheets are available at:
www.TriviaGameBooks.com

Player / Team Score Sheet

Name:_____

Preseason			Regular Season			Conference Tournament			Championship Game			Overtime Bonus	
1	26		1	26		1	26		1	26		1	
2	27		2	27		2	27		2	27		2	
3	28		3	28		3	28		3	28		3	
4	29		4	29		4	29		4	29		4	
5	30		5	30		5	30		5	30		5	
6	31		6	31		6	31		6	31		6	
7	32		7	32		7	32		7	32		7	
8	33		8	33		8	33		8	33		8	
9	34		9	34		9	34		9	34		9	
10	35		10	35		10	35		10	35		10	
11	36		11	36		11	36		11	36			
12	37		12	37		12	37		12	37			
13	38		13	38		13	38		13	38			
14	39		14	39		14	39		14	39			
15	40		15	40		15	40		15	40			
16	41		16	41		16	41		16	41			
17	42		17	42		17	42		17	42			
18	43		18	43		18	43		18	43			
19	44		19	44		19	44		19	44			
20	45		20	45		20	45		20	45			
21	46		21	46		21	46		21	46			
22	47		22	47		22	47		22	47			
23	48		23	48		23	48		23	48			
24	49		24	49		24	49		24	49			
25	50		25	50		25	50		25	50			
___x 1 =____			___x 2 =____			___x 3 =____			___x 4 =____			___x 4 =____	

Multiply total number correct by point value/quarter to calculate totals for each quarter.

Add total of all quarters below.

Total Points:_____

Thank you for playing *Blue Devilology Trivia Challenge*.

Additional score sheets are available at:
www.TriviaGameBooks.com